Intentional Living

Intentional Living

WRITINGS OF THOUGHTFUL CONSIDERATION FOR THE TRUE VALUE GAINED FROM LIVING LIFE WITH PURPOSE.

Dr. Drema Thompson

Xulon Elite

Xulon Press
2301 Lucien Way #415
Maitland, FL 32751
407.339.4217
www.xulonpress.com

© 2022 by Dr. Drema Thompson

All rights reserved solely by the author. The author guarantees all contents are original and do not infringe upon the legal rights of any other person or work. No part of this book may be reproduced in any form without the permission of the author.

Due to the changing nature of the Internet, if there are any web addresses, links, or URLs included in this manuscript, these may have been altered and may no longer be accessible. The views and opinions shared in this book belong solely to the author and do not necessarily reflect those of the publisher. The publisher therefore disclaims responsibility for the views or opinions expressed within the work.

Unless otherwise indicated, Scripture quotations taken from the English Standard Version (ESV). Copyright © 2001 by Crossway, a publishing ministry of Good News Publishers. Used by permission. All rights reserved.

Paperback ISBN-13: 978-1-66286-297-7
Ebook ISBN-13: 978-1-66286-298-4

This book is dedicated to:

The mission of encouraging those given a measure of faith, who are lost, or simply blinded right now from life's spinning wheel.

Table of Contents

Introduction xi
PART I: The Measure of a True Relationship 1
Low-Hanging Fruit 2
A Relationship to Have 4
Temporary Renderings 6
Borrowed Time 8
A Word for the Soul 10
Make Known the Path 12
Although the Barrier Was Breached 14
There Is Still a Safe Place 16
Almighty Grace Is Sufficient 18
Stepping into His Armor 20
Miracle in the Miracle 22
Secret Handshake 25
Declaring the Glory 26
Unwavering Walk 28
Walk in Destiny 30
Unto Him a Praise 32
The True Light 34
Not Alone in This Space 36
Strength in the Gifts 38
No Fear in Real Love 40
Seashells on the Shore 42
Ours to Claim 44
Out of Sync with the Plan 46

Powerless Is Our Will	48
Help My Unbelief	50
Out of the Shadow	52
Meaningful Engagement	55
A Song in My Heart	56
Ever Seeking His Presence	58
Lamented Hope	60
Comfort in Thee	62
Chosen	64
Help Is Near	66
True Love Is a Masterpiece	68
To Keep Him Near	70
A Secret Place	72
The Appointed Time	74
Phenomenal Walk with Thee	76
Patience in Love	78
The Unspoken Request	80
To Be Sealed	82
Time with the Father	84
Perfecting Will	86
Clarity in Purpose	88
Prayer of Trust	90
PART II: Foundation for Harsh Winds	93
Pyramid Building Structure	95
The Endless Well	96
Rainbow for All to See	98
Prepare Me	100
Moments in Time	102
In Him There Is Peace	104
He Will Sustain	106
Growing in Faith	108
Faith Though Fear Remain	110

Forward with Boldness of Faith 112
Christ Will Sustain 116
Looking Behind the Treasures. 118
Peace in the Season. 120
Ransom Paid 122
Restoration Still Lives 124
Sabbath Rest 126
The Breath Given 128
The Glory in the Veil 130
The Morning Dew 132
Value of My Portion. 134
When Faith Is Lost. 136
Faith Undivided 138
Choices 140
Christ's Life Is the Way 142
A Forever Kind of Love. 144
To Be Righteous 146
We Are Not Our Own. 148
When Darkness Presses Down 150
We Can Command 152
The Breath of Life. 154
PART III: Journey Through the Unknown 157
Coming into View 160
Deliverance 162
In the Promises 164
Live Like Only Today 166
Overflow Through the Struggle 168
The Samaritan's Example. 170
The Ten 172
Walking in Rain 174
Victory Is Ours 176
The Unending Reign 178

Along the Journey... 182
Carrying the Torch.. 184
Hold On to the Gift... 186
Kept in Christ... 188
Matchless Love.. 190
Moving through This Season...................................... 192
Nothing of This Earth Saves 194
Provision of Grace.. 196
Simply Walk Away.. 198
Speckled, Spotted, and Striped................................... 200
Under Heavenly Wings 202
Time Is Not Lost.. 204
Thorny Blessings.. 206
Reflections.. 209
About the Author... 211

Introduction

I CONGRATULATE YOU for taking a critical step by seeking all opportunities to search, identify, explore, and experience works that are intended to speak to your spiritual growth in God. The very purchase of this book is a signal to the Father of faith that you desire to utilize the time of grace that he has bestowed. Through His grace, we are extended a time to nurture and grow our relationship with Him as the cornerstone of our very existence—an existence in which our faith is challenged and increased to work in our favor.

Intentional Living is a collection of *I am*–inspired writings. I say *I am* because I began to experience early-morning awakenings that produced over one hundred writings within a very short period of time. You see, this could only have been via the hand of God. I had just managed to complete a grueling doctoral study that took over eight years to complete in 2020, and I did not want to pick up yet another book to read, let alone write anything at the time. These awakenings occurred around the 3:00 hour of the morning, as if I had slept a full eight hours. My eyes were wide open, and a restlessness came upon me. I simply had to get up and go to another room by myself. Often, I would move to the bathroom, where I would just sit and begin to read scriptures—and then one morning, I started writing. The writings seemed to come so effortlessly, and I would save them on my cell phone. As I began to share the writings with my husband, he made the declaration that I really needed to move them from my phone and get them to a place where they would not be lost. However, as I had done with other matters of *spiritualness*, I made a mental note, but I did not take any action to move them to a safe space.

One morning, my phone simply would not come on. I was in such a panic, that for a minute, I had not even thought about the writings, but I remembered that I had myriads of pictures saved to the phone of times spent with the grandbaby, and I became even more distressed. Then I realized that all the writings over the months would also be lost. My stress hit the level of panic at this point. I had saved neither the pictures nor the writings to a safe space; they were all on the device, and my fears mounted that they would be lost. I began to remove the protective coverings from the phone and placed it directly on the charging base for several hours. Going back to check on the phone, I could see that there was now a blue light, where there had previously been none.

After another hour or so, I retrieved the phone from the charger. I remember that, before I decided to press the power button, I murmured a short prayer that the Lord would force my phone to at least allow the data to be visible to access and transfer to a new phone. At the first press of the power button, there was nothing. The second time, I held the button for a few seconds longer, then the password screen came up and all the apps were visible. Immediately, but extremely carefully, I began to scroll through the phone to the saved files and saw both the pictures and the folder with the writings. Soon after, I exported both to my computer and began the process of really reviewing the writings. The possibility of losing these treasures prompted the compilation of this collection.

I want you to know that whatever God has placed in your view, thoughts, and spirit are a calling upon your life—for all our lives. To cultivate and activate what God has placed within, we must take intentional actions. The first is to seek God for wisdom, knowledge, and understanding in place of our one-mind fatigue and then wait through thought processes. The crazy thing about this for me is that not in my wildest imagination could anyone have told me I would write anything other than business articles about successful management or organizational behavior themes. After all, I have spent many years building a career in business administration for risk management in various industries. But therein is the beauty of God; He will use anybody to tell somebody about the living Savior, who can save everybody.

It is my prayer that this *Intentional Living Collection* will reveal a mustard seed treasure to many people—a treasure that allows a glimpse of who they are in, can become with, and their value to: Christ.

PART I:
The Measure of a True Relationship

YES, WE ARE to love as Jesus loved. At this point is where I will begin with the question: how did Jesus show His love?

In Him was life, and the life was the light of men (John 1:4). Jesus allowed His life to be used to bring life to all men. Knowing the significance of His work on Earth, Jesus did not hesitate, make excuses, seek an alternative path, or design His own plan from the plan of the Father, even after He came to a world that acted as if He was of no value to them. He was in the world, and the world was made through Him, yet the world could not identify Him upon sight, as indicated in John 1:10. Jesus became the standard.

Even if I am to be poured out as a drink offering upon the sacrificial offering of your faith, I am glad and rejoice with you all. Likewise, you also should be glad and rejoice with Me (Phil. 2:17–18). Jesus's life represented freedom. And as Moses lifted the serpent in the wilderness, so must the Son of Man be lifted that whoever believes in Him may have eternal life (John 3:14-15). Prior to Jesus, the method to overcome sin was sacrifice, a life for a wrong, as the means for atonement. This action provided the gravity of the weight of sin, that a life had to be given to overcome its impact. That the Father gave of Himself for the corrupt nature of man once and for all, is the true measure of love. His infinite love for us is expressed in taking on all our iniquities to be the last and ultimate sacrificial lamb that ever would need to be, making possible a true relationship with no defect or flaw.

Low-Hanging Fruit

KNOWING THE BEAUTY and sovereignty of a relationship with the Father, why is it so easy for man to wax cold and so very easy to get caught up in the day-to-day of this world that we live in? It's so obvious, yet for many, unknown. Upon awakening, *project death* begins. From our own consumption of knowing and hearing about the goings on in the world, we give wings to the death angel. We welcome him into our lives without even grasping that the actions we are taking are opening doors that we, by ourselves, have no power to shut. From the worries that we focus on to situations that involve our minds and hearts, we give rise to illness, anxiety, stress, and fear. Our very existence, right now, in this space, is preordained. No matter what station, or where you are right now in life, there is a divine appointment that you can either choose to move forward in alignment with the preparation or attempt to alter, circumvent, or eliminate the trajectory by any means necessary. This is an exposition into the choices that are being made every day that will frame how we accept or reject the helping hand that has been extended to us.

I will be the first to admit, each day I start off with the best intentions. I purpose, in my mind, that today is going to be a day that I maintain a mind of peace. At the time of this writing, a year or so has passed from the time that I began to experience a pain that was foreign to me on the left side of my abdomen. I say the pain was foreign because it was a feeling that I have never experienced prior to its onset. Everyone with whom I shared this newfound knowledge has eagerly encouraged me to seek medical attention. I acknowledge that I did choose initially to seek help from my primary care physician. Several x-rays were taken.

You see, my worst fears were that there would be a serious indication of a severe illness. In the multiple blood tests and x-rays that were taken, there were no visible signs of sickness or disease. In fact, at the time of the office visit, my blood pressure registered at the best level it had been in the last five years, and all other key blood indicators were within normal limits, except for one. When the medical provider noted my file, the comments read no indications, only slightly elevated lipids and a referral to have still more medical screening tests completed. All were done, without an earthly medical indication revealed.

Often, we experience seasons in life during which we feel hopeless. We know that the situation is progressing downward, but we cannot see a solution, or the pathway is covered, and we cannot see what steps to take or in what direction we should tread. It is my hope that, through the words that are included in this section, a flicker or spark of encouragement will result that causes you to seek out your own relationship with the Father who will come through in the known or unknown season.

A Relationship to Have

Greatest of wealth that one can amass
To the soul perceived the poorest at first glance
Makes no difference if the choices cast
Lead to a life left up to chance.

No check in steps taken or movement without direction
All signs of a life to be lost if no change in perspective
Rich or poor no baring to be
Only the heart that has been truly set free.

From the troubles and snares
Through a relationship unwavering
With the only one that truly loves and cares
So much so, His own He laid down.

A ransom, bail, and investment without guaranteed return
For us full payment, no balance due, or claim for a refund
Just a genuine walk with the Master each day
Spending quality time as He perfects the clay.

For God so loved the world, that He gave His only Son, that whoever believes in Him should not perish but have eternal life. For God did not send His Son into the world to condemn the world, but in order that the world might be saved through Him. Whoever believes in Him is not condemned, but whoever does not believe is condemned already, because He has not believed in the name of the only Son of God. And this is the judgment: the light has come into the world, and people loved the darkness rather than the light because their works were evil. For everyone who does wicked things hates the light and does not come to the light, lest his works should be exposed. But whoever does what is true comes to the light, so that it may be clearly seen that his works have been carried out in God.

—John 3:16–21

Temporary Renderings

The earthly buildups are not long-lasting.
Temporary renderings of limited things.
Yet, with every step along our decision tree,
Are the actions culminated from the things we feel, hear, and see?

Oh Lord, to be allowed to see beyond the stones and the veil
A world that exists in parallel,
Untouched, unshaken, unflawed.
From the ones in their infinite desires to unhinge me
Is the true essence of everything.

Though my heart is weary and unsettled,
I will continue to push on and seek Your wisdom
And knowledge to align better with your plan
Because you know what is truly best for me.

To find favor in the Master's hand
Is far beyond any earthly remarkable thing,
For His shaping and molding
Bring forth the very best of me.

Now the Lord is the Spirit, and where the Spirit of the Lord is, there is freedom. And we all, with unveiled face, beholding the glory of the Lord, are being transformed into the same image from one degree of glory to another. For this comes from the Lord who is the Spirit.

—2 Corinthians 3:17–18

Borrowed Time

Time is not ours for the taking.
If I said differently,
It would be just plain faking
With no guarantee for the next.

Second, minute, or hour, all borrowed;
Absolutely no guarantees that we will see tomorrow.
So, why so much focus on the things
That we can see and mindlessly say?

Moving through time as if no end
Because the mind is concentrated
In attaining abundance
Instead of a life lived abundantly each day.

With love, peace, joy, and contentment
The best phases we experience
Many at different intervals—
How to maintain them consistently.

Plagues so many
Until we invite God in
And let go of the flesh,
Its ups and downs in this earthly dimension and profound mess.

But we have this treasure in jars of clay, to show that the surpassing power belongs to God and not to us.

—2 Corinthians 4:7

A Word for the Soul

The age might be new;
Characters are the same, no matter who.
Either the walk is of God or
Earthly soles are molded to the shoes.

Whichever find passion and commit
With a force in all that you choose to do,
For the in-between will surely be worse for you.
Indecision, avoidance, and sheer lethargy

Are tools and trades that the enemy has prepared for thee;
Mountains of quicksand and valleys of fear
Along with a legion of excuses too.
Not right now; the way is not perfectly clear.

All things are not equal and neatly packed,
No ideas bound or stuck together like glue.
Wait, watch, and listen for the Holy Spirit.
In the stillness of the mind, God will come through

In the still, quiet place to center oneself in Christ.
For that is when the Holy Spirit appears and knows His role,
To reveal what is best
For the mind, body, and soul.

Be watchful, stand firm in the faith, act like men, be strong. Let all that you do be done in love.

—1 Corinthians 16:13–14

Make Known the Path

To be numbered among the lost
When the end descends
Is to have squandered all that God placed within reach;
His outstretched arms beckon one and all,

Especially those at heart that are meek.
No bolstering or championing
The successes that may appear to be,
Only true thankfulness and great fullness

For what God has done for you and me.
My life may not display as colorful as the onlookers contemplate me.
There may not be glimmers of light among the clay right now,
But with His perfecting touch and love, what gems we will grow to see!

For in His mission to find and save the missing,
Nothing grander can there be.
A love that transcends time's spinning wheel,
Even though, for the Master, not a minute too late for thee.

Behold, the fear of the Lord, that is wisdom, and to turn away from evil is understanding.

—Job 28:28

Although the Barrier Was Breached

The spoken Word that brought forth nothing into existence,
Then the preparation for the remaining foundation.
There were six days of labor
He put in the work for you and me

Yet the ancient ones could not see.
If they knew I would be here right now,
Would they have stood up for me?
Or would selfishness steal the day
As it did where He laid down his life on calvary?

For the love that God has for me,
He saw down the line the things
They could not see
And created a place just for me.

All found great in the plainness of view
The preparation for a tangible dwelling intended for us too,
A place in a garden set for a king
With no stress, worry, unrest, not of any kind or for anything.

But there in the yonder view,
A stranger, full of strife, grief, and willful disdain.
Yet, He knew my struggles would as such occur even today,
So much past the time the stone was rolled away.

How was it the barrier was breached,
As if that could keep the Master's loving arms so far out of our reach?
The goal is to be found upon higher ground,
Prepared and waiting for thee.

Love is patient and kind; love does not envy or boast; it is not arrogant or rude. It does not insist on its own way; it is not irritable or resentful; it does not rejoice at wrongdoing, but rejoices with the truth. Love bears all things, believes all things, hopes all things, endures all things. Love never ends.

—1 Corinthians 13:4–8

There Is Still a Safe Place

We all have our own antagonisms
That must receive our permissions,
Even when life seems to overcome.
Each day is a struggle to keep pace.
There is still a safe place.

For many, it is so simple to seek His face and pray.
Still others appear locked in rotation,
Swayed from the Master at the slightest irritation.
There is still a safe place.

At the surface, many things seem great.
All that takes precedence will wax thin our faith.
It is not to have nothing be bound,
But to not loose perspective.
There is still a safe place.

A focus on the I Am is where victory is found,
Even under the weight of earthly temptation.
All but to do is turn and seek refuge from His loving relation;
For that is where true wins surround.
There is still a safe place.

The beloved of the LORD dwells in safety. The High God surrounds him all day long, and dwells between his shoulders.

—Deuteronomy 33:12

Almighty Grace Is Sufficient

Slips, trips, stumbles, and falls,
For his grace is sufficient to cover them all.
These are not the ending to the story.
No, ma'am or sir, no, not at all!
They are simply occurrences that may befall.

Out of position, mindlessness erupts,
Anger, cruelty, and so much negative for us.
The chartered steps increasingly fade.
The air stiffens and blackness attempts to evade.

A soul full of frailty becomes easily shifted
Toward the negatives of an out-of-place mission.
Take care and continually glean all that is good.
Be a part of the solution,

Not an increaser of the enemy's delusion.
Let kindness and gentleness guide the decision.
Walk in position closely to the Master.
This is the sure way to head off a contrite spirit
Spiraling further toward disaster.

For you, O Lord, are good and forgiving, abounding in steadfast love to all who call upon you.
Give ear, O LORD, to my prayer; listen to my plea for grace.

—Psalm 86:5–6

Stepping into His Armor

Though we walk around free,
Many are incarcerated—
Not from the physical bars
And concrete floors and walls.

Our captors are the enemies' influence on people, places, and things,
Those that pierce us with their eyes of stone,
Tongues of cold steel that lash directly at our very faces
And ears that are tone-deaf to all that is said,

Places that we should not go,
Compelling us forward on toward the wrong way,
Creating visions filled with illusions
To a world that cares less and less with each passing day,

Things that scream out *Look at me*
To be elevated far above and for all to see
That add nothing of real value,
Just another trap for you and me.

The Word says: to keep a foot above, we have only to ask
From the Master, Lord, Savior, and friend
To help us chart the appropriate path;
Lord, help me to take on the whole armor of God and begin again.

Brothers, I do not consider that I have made it my own. But one thing I do: forgetting what lies behind and straining forward to what lies ahead, I press on toward the goal for the prize of the upward call of God in Christ Jesus. Let those of us who are mature think this way, and if in anything you think otherwise, God will reveal that also to you. Only let us hold true to what we have attained.

—Philippians 3:13–16

Miracle in the Miracle

Every uplifting thing
Is not a miracle in the making.
While there were countless that did and still today occur,
To focus on the miracle obscures heaven's door

And may lead us away
To focus on what has been and exists each day.
Even the disappointments and daily frustrations
With little contemplation on the work of the Savior

In the moment is truly living beyond what man can see or say,
Not to be confused or full of dismay.
Fret not for your circumstance or what
Miracle the enemy tells you will not come your way.

The miracle in the miracle is what I speak to you of today.
This form is only temporary
Though the mind is conditioned to think it all, and all
Thoughts of what and if we will miss any earthly thing

Render us mentally attached and subject to fall.
The miracle in the miracle is the Father knows and cares,
Not just the created vessel that we occupy,
But the very essence of what makes us individual.

With man it is impossible, but not with God. For all things are possible with God.

—Mark 10:27

Secret Handshake

IN THIS SECTION, the writings surround the joy and peace of the one special relationship and avoidance of distractions that impact mindful considerations in such a significant way. This type of distraction results when we allow people and things to take the place of Him in the heart. These are the cases in which the overwhelming legion is always present but unseen until it has taken a treacherous course. To avert the collision and impeding uncontrollable downward spiral, the focus is to become intentional in thought and deed to root out hidden agendas from within.

Motives defined by anything other than guided purpose lead to distorted actions and deeds. In 1 Timothy 3:16, the mystery of godliness without controversy holds to the truth that God fulfilled the written promises in the Word. Christ preached to the masses, and many believed His message until God received Him. The manifestation of the Word in the flesh was tried by the Spirit and witnessed in heaven by the angels. Yet, there were many in that moment who did not see nor understand, and this still rings true today.

The distractions are not permanent; it is the perseverance of the relationship with God that will stand. This example tells us our decisions are to be guided not only by motivations, but intentionality with clearly defined purpose. This is the focus of the writings that follow.

Declaring the Glory

Society moves and fashions
For some the *what, when,* and *where,*
Yet to be on target for your true *why*
Is to have seen and experienced
The joy that only God can give.

For a soul that is truly blowing in the wind
Has only to look beyond the veil.
Seek the pathway that is guided by the true light.
Even the earth yet reveals His hidden treasures
That lead to His intentions.

For the blossoms in early spring
To the Crayola leaf array in the fall of the year
All provide a visual point of reference
Of the Lord's greatness to revere
For our purpose and the very best pleasures.

Things that come to shake up our view
For moments of reflection during the journey
To reach a walk with the Trinity,
As nothing and no one can whisper
Influences of your *what, where,* and *when* ever again,
Because He has kept us from within.

Better is a little with righteousness than great revenues with injustice.

—Proverbs 16:8

Unwavering Walk

A step toward the wrong in any way
Is not the end for a chest that inflates.
The opportunity for correction
Is shrouded in His love, mercy, and grace.

While we have unlimited potential,
It is not time limitless.
As with any competition,
We must strive to keep pace
For the final test.

He never foretold our course would be easy
Or filled with successes.
For that, we have input
To shape our progressions.

When temptation is allowed entry into this life,
It is not the ending to have strife.
Only the Master sees past the test;
That is why an unwavering connection is best.

You shall love the Lord your God with all your heart and with all your soul and with all your strength and with all your mind, and your neighbor as yourself.

—Luke 10:27

Walk in Destiny

A reflection of perfection are we.
To only acknowledge the depth
And breadth of just this one thing
Is to walk in the very essence of our destiny,

Free from the cares of this side of being,
Fulfilling the Master's perfect will and plan in season,
To walk as if nothing else has meaning,
But taking each step as guided without stealing.

Away with hearts cold and unfeeling.
Toward the Father, open-hearted, and focused on knowing.
The path was paved oh, so long ago;
Only the remnant of the remnant understands so.

How do we navigate this world so uncaring?
It becomes necessary to spread and not conceal
A growing heart full of endless love and sharing,
One only a walk with the Savior can reveal.

For we do not wrestle against flesh and blood, but against the rulers, against the authorities, against the cosmic powers over this present darkness, against the spiritual forces of evil in the heavenly places. Therefore, take up the whole armor of God, that you may be able to withstand in the evil day, and having done all, to stand firm.

—Ephesians 6:12–13

Unto Him a Praise

During the creation was an opportunity in the making.
Although His greatest being would lose position
Beyond any measure possibly to be conceived,
With matchless love, He came and lived.

A crucifixion for you and me.
With the breath I have this day,
I thank him even with insufficiency of the words I know to say:
Thank you, Lord, for Your sacrifice.

With a thousand tongues all in unison,
Still not enough even alone for just me.
Thank you, Lord, for Your mercy and grace
That did not have to be.

Beyond the capacity of my feeble mind,
No tongues or expression reflect adequately
How this life we live has no measure of success
That can equate to what was done on Calvary.

As for you, O LORD, you will not restrain your mercy from me; your steadfast love and your faithfulness will ever preserve me!

—Psalm 40:11

The True Light

During my moments of indifference,
Please place Your Spirit in my path
To move me from the darkness
To the light and life of the visible.

Where our connection becomes strong
Once again, as though no division,
Lord, grant me a peace and serenity
That will open my voice to exalt thee,

One that shouts to the rooftops above
And yells the gratefulness
I have for all to see
How wonderful and beautiful is Your love for me!

A broken vessel marred in so many ways,
Far beyond what everyone sees each day,
That with Your Spirit pouring out mercy and grace,
So much so that it shapes my vision of your face.

God is our refuge and strength, a very present help in trouble.

—Psalm 46:1

Not Alone in This Space

Upon two tablets laid out the plan
Direction for yesterday, today, and tomorrow's insurrection.
To allow us to be found upright and stand,
A purpose and will shroud within the concrete,

A true testimony made for continual review and reflection,
Not the opaqueness and transparencies we often speak and profess
That so many are disillusioned with
In clearing their own weighted chests,

Only to genuinely love no animosity, hatred, or stress,
Despite the circumstances for which we are found
Or the strategic encampments that too often abound,
But an armor filled from the top to the bottom

That has no chinks or areas of distress.
The fortification, if penetrated, still yet
Have we the Master's mercy and grace.
For alone is impossible, only through
The welcoming of Him and His Holy Spirit in this space.

So we have come to know and to believe the love that God has for us. God is love, and whoever abides in love abides in God, and God abides in him.

—1 John 4:16

Strength in the Gifts

A heart that is full of love
There is an overwhelming joy.
Vessels of strength that are at peace
That are intentional with overflowing kindness.

Seeking only to exude goodness
Along a journey marked by unwavering faithfulness
With care to ensure every act with gentleness
And having the ultimate in self-control,

For all of these are the gifts that come
When continual walk with God is your goal,
Allowing the Holy Spirit to guide and hold.

Now there are varieties of gifts, but the same Spirit; and there are varieties of service, but the same Lord; and there are varieties of activities, but it is the same God who empowers them all in everyone. To each is given the manifestation of the Spirit for the common good.

—1 Corinthians 12:4–7

No Fear in Real Love

Love is not truly just a four-letter word;
In many ways, it is severely misunderstood.
True love is showered on those that are not good.
When the pain creeps in, it excels to the umpteenth degree

In so doing it surrounds you but envelops me
For that is the love
God wanted to be
That we love one another unconditionally.

This is not a feat that we can accomplish on our own
But a journey with hills, mountains, and deep valleys below
Some we will find easy and others extreme.

But in His love for us
We are equipped for both and anything in-between.
It is my prayer that we recognize whose and who we are
Indeed, my friend, we are a blessed people

Which nothing and none can take away
The Master's perfect gift for you and me
A love beyond the eyes of the heart
And anything that we can see.

You shall love the Lord your God with all your heart and with all your soul and with all your mind. This is the great and first commandment. And a second is like it: You shall love your neighbor as yourself.

—Matthew 22:37–40

Seashells on the Shore

Three seashells lying upon the shore,
One appears to have no desire for anything more,
Burrowing deeply in the sand we find
The inhabitant had long left its covering for better accommodations
And in its isolation no one sought it out to carry.

Another reflects the beaming sunlight
Although not by purpose and intention
Merely through the opulence of its outer covering
A reflection that disappears
Upon the sun descending and reflects no more.

Yet the other was found upside down
With an opening that appeared waiting to be filled
As if to beckon a new inhabitant
With true purpose and goodwill.

Of the three seashells, which one is thee?
The first with no desire or care
To be of use or value by the King,
The second a mere reflection
No depth, just an outer skin and surface to be seen,

Or the last of the three
Upward-facing and waiting
A vessel deep and wide
Wanting and willing to be filled
To use your gifts for His perfect plan and will.

We know that for those who love God, all things work together for good, for those who are called according to His purpose.

—Romans 8:28–29

Ours to Claim

Lord, my focus sometimes wanes;
My love for Thee yet remains.
To be intentional is the goal
Toward a purposeful life in Christ
Who seeks to claim lost souls.

Help me, oh God.
Show me Your will and way
That I may recognize
The enemy's traps laid each day.

Teach me. Lord, to know
What is of Thee
That my heart will be weary
Of the pathway to defeat.

Guide me to be intentional during the wait
That an outward image of my journey
Just might help others along their way.
To that end, mold my mind to focus

With spiritual eyes, ears, and lips
That I might see, hear, and sow
Righteous seeds with clarity in aim,
Encouraging that to overcome is ours to claim.

For there is no distinction: for all have sinned and fall short of the glory of God, and are justified by His grace as a gift, through the redemption that is in Christ Jesus.

—Romans 3:22–24

Out of Sync with the Plan

To be in alignment with God is the goal
For in this purpose will decide the direction of the soul.
Being one with the Master's perfect will
Although it is often difficult
To remain humble and keep still.

The assaults stack up one by one.
Often, we are unawares caught
Too engrossed in the day-to-day
To recognize and identify the enemy in play
For it is exactly that to Him.

A game of chance
To change your life's destiny
Because the enemy cannot on his own win,
So why are so many wildernesses bound
With the greatest navigation system to be found.

The answer is not so simple you see
Because it involves foregoing the will of you and me
That is right those freedoms we constantly seek
Doing the things in the manner we wish
Saying whatever we choose to speak.

Not acknowledging His sovereignty
The perfect will and plan
That from the spoken words of life
Has been ours to claim
Since the earth began.

The LORD will keep you from all evil; He will keep your life. The LORD will keep your going out and your coming in from this time forth and forevermore.

—Psalm 121:7–8

Powerless Is Our Will

Oh, Holy God, if You please
Carry me along this journey.
Be the director of this life
Chart the pathway and refine the course.

To discover my win
Move me from what mine eyes can see
Toward all that You have for me.
Clarity of mind to identify the separation

That comes with a life filled with sin
Purity of heart to not drown in frustration
Humbleness of spirit to draw others near
To speak of Your goodness.

And proclaim emancipation
From the enemy's devices
And efforts to kill
All the goodness that comes from having You within.

Therefore, my beloved, as you have always obeyed, so now, not only as in my presence but much more in my absence, work out your own salvation with fear and trembling, for it is God who works in you, both to will and to work for His good pleasure.

—Philippians 2:12–13

Help My Unbelief

Oh, how my soul thirsts for thee
Even when I am blind and cannot see.
The road ahead becomes blurry
Your steps and the path seem vague to me.

Though I try to convince myself I know the way
With each new day, I fade farther away.
Help me, Oh God, to pivot correctly
Not too fast or too slow but in alignment with Your perfect plan and direction.

Teach me, Oh God, Your perfect will.
Help me to recognize when I must be still.
Show me what is best for each new sunshine;
Breath on me that fears blow away.

Help my unbelief that creeps in each day.
To be in alignment with the Son's direction is what I desire.
Even though the clay must be burned in the fire,
I know ultimately the Word will withstand, cure, and fulfill all desires.

And Jesus said to him, 'If you can'! All things are possible for one who believes.

—Mark 9:23

Out of the Shadow

Out of the shadows, He can only call;
Nothing in your works has strength
Only His love, mercy, and grace.
How can we see the truth and the light?
This world is a crazy place.

Make it your purpose;
Invest in a strong tower that seeks nothing from you
Showers only His love, mercy, and grace.
Will we see the truth and the light?
This world is a crazy place.

Turn your focus on the Guiding Light
Let the power of the Holy Spirit show through
Brings only His love, mercy, and grace.
There is the truth and the light
This world is a crazy place.

Our actions show our belief and faith
No works will erase a heart impure
Nothing can take His place
He is full of love, mercy, and grace
When will we see the truth and the light?
This world is a crazy place.

Out of the shadow, longing no more
Living a life through His righteousness we endure.
He is full of love, mercy, and grace.
Now we can see the truth and the light.
This world is a crazy place.

Whoever pursues righteousness and kindness will find life, righteousness, and honor.

—Proverbs 21:21

Meaningful Engagement

ON MY JOURNEY to achieve a doctorate, one of the highest forms of ascension to superior earthly knowledge was a requirement to exemplify that my years of study culminated in a supreme level of understanding of the subject matter. The time had come to demonstrate the gained knowledge and complete an original research study. The institution defined parameters for the study within a rubric. The rubric included details defining the minimum requirements for each section of the study. Within each section, there were required elements. The elements were to be presented with a scholarly tone and succinct contextual language. Throughout the research journey, multiple external connection points occurred where others' (superior in knowledge) worldviews and perspectives were injected at various intervals with the sole intent to challenge and refine the completed work to ensure integrity of the research process and the outcomes.

Often today, our outcomes evolve, absent measured purpose, qualified refinement, and thoughtful inspection, and are guided strictly by motives to achieve rather than by mindful evolution that knows He is real, sight unseen. The storing up of the Lord's work is a critical component to our salvation (Ps. 119:11). May grace and peace be exponentially multiplied to those in the knowledge of God for the avoidance of sin against the Father (2 Pet. 1:2). After years of scholarly writing and culmination of achieving the highest earthly academic goal, the writings that follow are inspired from my relationship with the Father, His Word, and personal mindful reflection of the achievement and how the Holy Spirit ushered me through. It is my prayer that they may be seeds sprinkled wherever fertile ground abounds.

A Song in My Heart

He knows me best
Successes, disappointments, and failures
And a barrage of all the rest
The shortcomings, one and all.

Even the laugh, smile, and cry,
Although I forget to call
To ask not a shear travesty
Though I cannot foretell tomorrow.

Or any second beyond the present moment I see
There is still so much promise deep down inside of me
To allow the filling of the urns
Is still our choice short of the cracked sky and His return?

To a world so lost and lifeless be
Fueling generations' turn from the King
Cries of me and acknowledgment of what I want to be
Despite the spoken Word so long ago
To the ancestors and all to see.

For I know the plans I have for you, declares the LORD, plans for welfare and not for evil, to give you a future and a hope.

—Jeremiah 29:11

Ever Seeking His Presence

A word from the sacred one
A gift to be bestowed
But only for those
Whose ears are pricked to hear.

A heart open and ready to be filled
Is the true blessing for the soul.
The question is quite clear;
How do so many obtain it?

Yet many never claim it
Even when the Word became whole
Where to begin if you want in
The I Am provided the blueprint.

It is not complicated to comprehend
Find your nourishment in the Word
A supper used to teach
Of the true goal to reach.

Intentional purpose guiding your direction
Your ultimate choosing
The plan for salvation
Pushing aside the peripheral.

Even when the heart is tinged
Ever seek His presence
In the still, quiet place where He waits
For it is only there that love, joy, and peace live.

For everyone who calls on the name of the Lord will be saved.

—Romans 10:13

Lamented Hope

The Master is never far off from thee;
He seeks out from the places we cannot see
Never by pull force or push actions toward you and me
A purposeful wind that seeks to make us free.

Sometimes it seems as though solitary
When the truth lies behind the tares of the enemy
Stress nor fret remove the thorns
Only to bury them further along.

Seeking the Comforter to clear the fog
Is only to settle and center oneself amid it all.
To settle is to welcome the Father in the secret places
To root out division within the mental spaces
It is a focus on being intentional

And form the bond that is not accidental.
A bond built on love, faith, and trust
Only secured by the Spirit's guidance,
Master's hand, and God's bountiful love for all of us.

But God shows His love for us in that while we were still sinners, Christ died for us.

—Romans 5:8

Comfort in Thee

Lord, I take comfort in Thee
Even though most times I cannot see
The scales try to obscure my view
Yet You beckon me to come to You.

Just as I am a heart stained
Bringing nothing, only receiving Your love
Asking nothing from above
Only to Yours I am to be claimed

To be included when You return
With pierced side and nail-stretched hands;
Guide me, Oh God, through to the end.

We lay open our hearts for your excision;
Help us to guard our thoughts and decisions.
We have but one opportunity and this life will end
Help us, oh God, to garner composure.

To ensure when the cloud is burst through
We can hold our heads upright
Not hide among the stones
And feel unwelcomed and fear
In loving view of the return of our Savior
As He draws near.

So now faith, hope, and love abide, these three; but the greatest of these is love.

—1 Corinthians 13:13

Chosen

The light within that will burn bright
Only to be dimmed by the sin-filled life
Even to willful wrongdoing
There a mercy seat review

An opportunity, a chance, a decision
We all must one day go through.
Earthly living should not our heart behold
A heavenly trajectory be the focus for the soul

Where peace, joy, and true happiness abound
In the presence of God can this only be found.
So why so many relish in the wilderness
The enemy's guile fools the very elect?

Just one moment
Not purposeful in intent
Creates the crevice
A chink in the mind's armor

To move us from the knowledge of the victor.
The battle already won
With the unselfish sacrifice
A gift so complete only accomplished by the Son.

But if we walk in the light, as He is in the light, we have fellowship with one another, and the blood of Jesus His Son cleanses us from all sin.

—1 John 1:7

Help Is Near

Push past overriding thoughts of sadness and fears
For He is holy and the very essence
Of all that is needed so one must focus
Another day and true victory draws near.

For what do we truly have here on this earth
But the wrath, regret, and envy of the jealous one?
Fight through the disappointment and pain;
Push past the discouragement and disdain.

Allow the One who was prepared for this fight
To take over and guide us through,
For His way is always right.
Live each day in His presence

For in Him is the light.
Live each day in His presence
For in Him is the light.
Live each day in His presence
To gain the strength needed to persevere.

Do not be conformed to this world, but be transformed by the renewal of your mind, that by testing you may discern what is the will of God, what is good and acceptable and perfect.

—Romans 12:2

True Love Is a Masterpiece

If my love for you
Could paint a picture,
It would be a masterpiece
With what the Master has placed inside.

I love you beyond the limits
Of what I can see.
It is His love where it all begins
And only His love

Will chart the true course until the end,
An unconditional love
That has no bounds
Wrapped in the Master's mercy and grace,

Is a love that no one
Or anything can replace.
Why then is the world in such a state
If it is only the love

Of the Master is what it really takes?
To some the solution is so simple
Yet for many overly complex
You see this love is
Humility, forgiveness, forbearance, and forgetting all the rest.

No temptation has overtaken you that is not common to man. God is faithful, and He will not let you be tempted beyond your ability, but with the temptation He will also provide the way of escape, that you may be able to endure it.

—1 Corinthians 10:13

To Keep Him Near

Everything He doeth, it is well.
There was a plan from the very beginning
A process, a methodology, and reason
Just because right now we are reeling in this season
It does not mean the course is no more.

It simply means to continue on the road;
The connection must be strengthened.
Our link to Him must include purpose and precision.
To see the path that He charted ahead,
Focus your heart and seek Him in prayer.

For did thee not also take the time to measure this earth
Place the footings on which the foundation lays
As the members shouted in unison
And proclaimed glory to His name:
Lord, we ask the scales to be excised from our eyes?

The muffle from our ears
And the chains from the heart
To release the proclamations from our mouths
That will ensure our ever-mindfulness
To seek Thee and keep You near.

For if while we were enemies we were reconciled to God by the death of His Son, much more, now that we are reconciled, shall we be saved by His life.

—Romans 5:10

A Secret Place

In the secret place
There I seek Thy face
To gain that which is
In a perfect plan and will

As shared so very long ago
A purpose and destination guided
By the Trinity undivided
To make me whole.

Unchanged from yesterday
Beyond the error of my ways
Past present and future
To save my soul.

To be included in the final story
That all may proclaim
Hallelujah to the Savior
The victor before there ever was.
Glory, to the King of Kings.

Seek the LORD and His strength; seek His presence continually!
—1 Chronicles 16:11

The Appointed Time

To have patience is to know the Master
For in your time spent with Him reveals the pathway from disaster.
Even though calamity may befall
He reigns supreme above anything and all.

A walk in His presence removes the world's cares
For He picks us up and all the dead weight we bear.
To be one with the Holiest of Holy
Is the solemn goal
For in the relationship lies the rest for the wearied soul.

Even though time seems to evaporate and waste
Not a second, minute, hour, day, week, month, nor year
Are meant to be spent
Wondering or worrying about earthly snares.

Give it all over to the one with the knowledge of the plan
Who knows the beginning and ending of man
Then wait, watch, and be still
And see your deliverance in accordance with His will.

Rejoice in hope, be patient in tribulation, be constant in prayer.

—Romans 12:12

Phenomenal Walk with Thee

To be used by God is a phenomenal occurrence
An instrument made by and built for the use of the true King.
Nothing could ever possibly contain the joy from just His presence
How great and auspicious is such a thing.

To have a love that no one can contain
A joy that trumps any earthly offering,
The peace that calms the deep blue sea
A walk with the Father that transcends all humanly connections for you and me.

Why so hard to grasp a hold
Especially when His ultimate delivery is to save the soul
Marred in yesterday's chatter, today's calamity, and future frivolous matters.

We shrink away from the true source that can make us whole.
A word please, Master, if You please,
Help me to make wise decisions and strengthen my belief
For these are the enemies of the evil one that are too easily let go.

Let us hold fast the confession of our hope without wavering, for He who promised is faithful.

—Hebrews 10:23

Patience in Love

The grace of the Father
Is beyond anything in our sight.
His patience endures all our worst
Even those in our egregious might.

He does not linger in our iniquities
Or second-by-second disdains.
His love is ever-forgiving and refreshing
Like the dew left from a morning rain.

His hands are outstretched welcoming us in
Like a true Father would,
Even as our hearts are filled with sin
A rapture so great to cover the stains.

In it our victory from this earthly realm
To see Him manifest within our touch
Is a glory to the Father
Who truly loves each one of us.

More than that, we also rejoice in God through our Lord Jesus Christ, through whom we have now received reconciliation.

—Romans 5:11

The Unspoken Request

No prayer is a request unspoken;
Each day of the journey
When we fail to ask of Him
The guidance lost becomes so great

And so easy to lose sight of Him.
Just a moment without focus
On the crowd both near and far
Is where it all begins.

The first strike to change a heart
From the direction, vision, and comfort of knowing
The feet on the right path
That was laid so very long ago.

The importance of faith and increased belief
The continued teachings at His feet
Help them to know with each passing day
It is never a good thing not to pray.

Do not be anxious about anything, but in everything by prayer and supplication with thanksgiving let your requests be made known to God. And the peace of God, which surpasses all understanding, will guard your hearts and your minds in Christ Jesus.

—Philippians 4:6–7

To Be Sealed

Dear Lord, help me to see
The true enemy in me
That I walk the pathway without falter
And help as many as I can along the way
Through Jesus's steps, paved to follow.

Lord, help me to know
That my decisions can spark or halt my growth
And that my life has true meaning far broader
Than any earthly entanglement presents.
For these I must descend

To allow Your Word in the space
To accept today Your love, mercy, and grace
For in this life no guaranteed tomorrow.
Holy Spirit, guide, I plead
In my mind open a renewed need
That will reveal the true seed.

Dear Lord, help me to see
The true enemy in me
That seeks to cloud progress.
No death can attest that which has already been addressed and revealed;
Oh Lord, in my mind, place Your seal.

If any of you lacks wisdom, let him ask God, who gives generously to all without reproach, and it will be given him.

—James 1:5

Time with the Father

To walk with God
Is to know Him.
To know God
Is to Love Him.
To love God
Is to spend time with Him.

In the secret place
Where no one dwells
There is where to find Him
Gently waiting for the appointed time
That is set aside just for Him.

As a child clamoring for your attention
So too, we must be for the Holy One
Beyond this dimension
Watching, waiting, ever listening.

For the Master's voice
Beyond the chatter of this universe
A sound so marvelous
In the mind's ear shear melodious
And time spent oh so precious.

For by grace you have been saved through faith. And this is not your own doing; it is the gift of God, not a result of works, so that no one may boast.

—Ephesians 2:8–9

Perfecting Will

If salvation is the only reason we praise,
Then what of His love He freely gave,
A love transcending from generation to generation
For all His children, no matter the station
A love that covers all our weaknesses?

Unlike the effect of the enemy's will
To kill, in and out of season,
You know all that we invest in those walking on land,
As if they hold salvation in the palms of their hands.
Yes, salvation is a perfect goal.

Yet falling in love with Jesus
Is what truly saves the soul,
This remarkable love that can open any door
To a world where the Savior appears

To us in real time more and more,
When prayers are spoken
And His answers are already in route
Because of believing in the Master's
plan and perfect will for you.

For this is the will of God, that by doing good you should put to silence the ignorance of foolish people.

—1 Peter 2:15

Clarity in Purpose

Lord, you have cleared a pathway for me
Even though with my bare eyes I cannot see.
Help me, Lord, in the walk
That my very essence would be found pregnant
With the knowledge of Thee

So much so I would embody
The strongest imagery
Of a life vibrant and free
That no one might ever divide
The heart in-between.

Impress upon me each day a new focus
Targets to improve and chip away
Thorns that encase and try to impede
The shaping of a life that seeks to obey.

Lord, grant the serenity of a union with the Trinity
Beyond my pain, frustrations, and dismay
To an armor that fulfills the promises granted
On a hill far away, that most glorious day.

And He will be the stability of your times, abundance of salvation, wisdom, and knowledge; the fear of the LORD is Zion's treasure.

—Isaiah 33:6

Prayer of Trust

There are many things in this life
That I do not understand,
But with unblinded trust
I yet place my hand in Your hand.

An open vessel I want to be
That can be filled and used by You
Beyond anything I could ever imagine
Or ever thought for me.

In the beginning a divine plan
A perfect will that considers the complete story
And does not blot me out so quickly
After my stumbles, slips, and slides from glory.

Lord, teach me to look past my own comprehension;
Help me navigate this dimension
To be humble within whatever lot or degree
That is used to perfect and make the best out of me.

Lord, I will trust in You
Even for the things not seen
Or for the today and what may seem
For from the beginning, a master plan was made for me;
Lord, I trust You with everything.

Keep steady my steps according to Your promise, and let no iniquity get dominion over me.

—Psalm 119:133

PART II:
Foundation for Harsh Winds

Relationships in this life are not always easy. For a successful relationship, thoughtful engagement is necessary, time must be exhausted, sacrifices must be made to ensure consistency, and, most importantly, an appropriate foundation is needed. Like any foundation, it does not just materialize. For over fifteen years, I had the responsibility for managing property and casualty insurance compliance for mortgage-backed securities. One of the functions of the role involved an understanding of property preservation, minimizing the lender's fiscal responsibility. During this time, I was exposed to elements of home construction that were impactful to my understanding of the importance of my role in the restitution process. When a house is built, there is the idea or purpose for how the house will be used. The idea or purpose is translated into a blueprint or rendering of each facet of the building from the materials that will be sourced to the people and skills needed to move forward.

The builder and homeowner move forward in faith that the structure will stand. During the phases of the build, the area or ground is excavated in preparation for footings. The footings are leveled either for wood framing or poured cement to form the foundation. Either material used must be level and shore up the remaining structure of the house, occupants, and their belongings. The foundation is one of the more costly components of the build. As such, the foundation must be solid.

Luke 4 paints a picture of what can be achieved when one has God's Word as the foundation for life, clearly defined purpose, and consistent intentionality. Jesus had been taught the Word of God and exercised the knowledge that was given. Luke 4:1 indicates Jesus was full of the Holy Spirit and was led in the Spirit into the wilderness to endure forty days of temptation.

Jesus ate nothing; He only lived by the Word. When the temptation came, His house was already shored up by an unmovable and unshakeable foundation. When the temptations came, though hungry, He had received the necessary nourishment to sustain Him during the trial.

The house, as a structure, has an intended purpose. It is a place of shelter from the elements. Its stability is reliant upon a solid foundation. Our relationships must have an intended purpose. The relationship is designed to add to our existence and not be a detraction. As a result, the foundation of our relationships becomes critical. The author writes, For God so loved the world, He gave His only begotten Son, that whosoever will believe in Him shall not perish but have everlasting life (John 3:16).

The foundation for love starts with the Father. Even from creation, the Father qualified His love with intentional actions. Man was not merely spoken into existence. There was a blueprint that included specificity. The full essence of God was involved in the process. From my feeble summation, the Lord purposed in His reasoning to create a being, but not just any being. The being was to be a creation that was likened unto Him in form. Then with His touch, man was crafted and shaped with specificity, and the breath of God imparted into the creation—a giving of Himself that only He can take away. What an example of the perfect foundation for a true relationship.

Pyramid Building Structure

IN OUR RELATIONSHIP, we reflect on God's mercy and grace and intentionality for us. We often feel the stares when we go out with friends, attend church services, and take part in family gatherings. We ponder what it is that makes our relationships stand out among many. We have been told on various occasions that it was obvious that we really love one another, or she really loves him, and he really loves her. It was obvious that no one was going to come between us, no matter what. While those words to some may appear to represent comments about a loving couple that are *all in* for each other, we propose an alternative assessment. In our assessment, we found that the minute we stopped relying on us and put us in the hands of God, we began to experience less of the very same ups and downs that will create havoc in the best of relationships. This does not mean that we have accomplished it all; by far, it means that we have acknowledged to one another that, individually, we can either choose to stand and continue the fight against one another or at any given point in time one of us will choose to lie down. And no, we do not keep count how frequently one decides to retreat over the other.

For instance, on a windy day, depending upon your vantage point, the wind can be said to blow from east to west. If you use your point of orientation and turn your back, the wind will appear to be blowing west to east. Often during colder months, you can see children playing outside. As a gust of wind occurs, you will see them turn their backs almost instinctively. The turned backs are not for the purpose of trying to isolate themselves from one another. The children have faith to endure the cold, as they do not retreat; they take a brief opportunity to redirect the impact of a frigid wind from the sensitive skin on the face to an area that is covered and shielded. The fact is the wind did not change its direction; the children changed their orientation. The wind was truly blowing from east to west. In the choice to lie down, one of us simply moves forward in faith and changes our orientation in the face of a strong rushing wind, even those of our own making.

In this section, the writings surround the joy and peace of the one special relationship because of His intentional foundation, the importance of growing your faith in making intentional plans to nurture that relationship and move forward despite the harsh winds that will blow.

The Endless Well

There are many vessels to occupy when the water is poured:
Some that are damaged and accept but leaks abound
Others too full to accept an ounce of anything more
Many that continually accept as a well with no floor.

No matter the vessel the water yet remains
Is ever present and ready to be poured
Never running out as it flows through heaven's door
All that is required is to have the tiniest of faith.

In all that the Savior did with His birth, life, and death to save us,
Not a requirement but a sacrifice
A decision, choice, and mission
To reclaim and restore what was stolen with strife.

The leaking vessel understands but holds no belief
The full vessel simply chooses not to receive
A vessel that accepts and overflows is what I long to be;
From the overflow, someone else may strengthen me.

The LORD is my strength and my shield; in Him my heart trusts, and I am helped; my heart exults, and with my song I give thanks to Him.

—Psalm 28:7

Rainbow for All to See

If I lose sight of the spiritual plane
The field can produce no fruit.
All that will be left is the wasting-away and dying roots.
No longer a blade that stands the test of time
Dried up and shelved with others in kind.

But with the Master's loving touch
I march on despite the mess that is me.
Onward clothed in His victory
One that began so many sins before
Leading the way to each safe door.

Try as I must to stay in The Way
So many challenges, struggles, and disappointments appear each day.
While these are par for the course and to be expected
Without the full of His armor so easy to become infected.

This is but a temporary station
Live, love, laugh, and pray without restriction
Foregoing the assailant's works of confliction.
For God has, is, and will always be
Supreme above all said seen or heard;

Yes, everything.

Finally, be strong in the Lord and in the strength of His might.
—Ephesians 6:10

Prepare Me

Lord, prepare me for the rain;
Lord, prepare me for the pain;
Oh Lord, prepare me for the harvest to come.
Help me, Oh God, to keep Your Word engrained.
Help me, Oh God, to keep Your Word engrained.

People angry acting near and far
Seems time is rapidly moving by, yet the Word says for You no change,
And I know You reign.
Yes, I know You reign.

Lord, prepare me for the rain;
Lord, prepare me for the pain;
Oh Lord, prepare me for the harvest to come.
Help me, Oh God, to keep Your Word engrained.
Help me, Oh God, to keep Your Word engrained.

From day to day though attempts to toss us here and there
The Word promises You will not change;
The Lord will always reign;
Yes, I know You reign.

Lord, prepare me for the rain;
Lord, prepare me for the pain;
Oh Lord, prepare me for the harvest to come.
Help me, Oh God, to keep Your Word engrained.
Help me, Oh God, to keep Your Word engrained.

The Lord will always reign;
Yes, I know You reign.

Sow for yourselves righteousness; reap steadfast love; break up your fallow ground, for it is the time to seek the LORD, that He may come and rain righteousness upon you.

—Hosea 10:12

Moments in Time

If your neighbor whom you do not really know
Lost sight and could not see the road,
Would your outstretched hands reach for and carry the load
Or in mind be oblivious and tend only to thee?

Moving and grooving in thine own misery
Healing of the nation becomes increasingly distant
With life choices that ignore the true mission
One's walking for the many cannot will the change.

Only through the magnificent power that His love brings
Even when death comes and brings so much pain
Heartache abounds like never-ending rain
Disappointment and letdowns seem to stifle the breath.

Moments in time stand still
And the dawn of a new day seems light-years away
The Father may move aside for reasons unknown
But in the faith can we only weather the storm.

No matter the strength of winds rushing on with intensity
Only through Him can we endure to the ending
For those who choose not to obey
That is the neighbor for whom we must pray.

So, whatever you wish that others would do to you, do also to them, for this is the Law and the Prophets.

—Matthew 7:12

In Him There Is Peace

Trouble in this world is no secret;
This was foretold of its existence long ago.
All but to open the eyes each morning to see it,
Yet so many take the time each day
To welcome it in and greet it.

Engraving the negative on the mind's heart
Reveling in the potential impact of loss and strife
When our time limits, He does not receive it.
We dismiss the value of the Master's win
And usher faith out and allow trouble in.

Being human beings in this life
So much more value does the daily breath bring.
When you do not take within and receive it
Then trouble takes its rightful place
When no belief, there is no space.

To embrace all the commotion and chatter
During a time when real strength
Needed to sustain comes from the latter.
Allowing in the Master
From the very small to the greatest of matters.

Before they call, I will answer; while they are yet speaking, I will hear.

—Isaiah 65:24

He Will Sustain

Father, I treasure my connection to Thee
Even though through cloudy eyes
And mind filled with lethargy.
You are and have been on my side
And will always be.

Day by day is the only way to see
Beyond the peaks, hills, and valleys
A view of something so much greater
Only those in tune push aside the now for later.

A synchronized appointment
In the not-too-distant future
Where the cares of this moon
Shall no longer a light be cast.

For the impact will no longer
Shake the will, shape the heart,
Nor chop away at the stone,
For Your Word has already made it known.

Wait for the LORD; be strong, and let your heart take courage; wait for the LORD!

—Psalm 27:14

Growing in Faith

It has never been a focus on doing
While our works are actions of believing.
It is far better to have self-control in choosing
To be on the right side in the conclusion.

Though He gives us liberty and free will
The expected decision is not always visible.
In this life so many influences, obstacles, and detours.
So much pressure to veer off-course

Yet we have an infinite supplier of peace and joy
If only we give up the physical and rely on the Creator
Not just at the surface but from the essence of our being
There we will receive the power to persevere.

It is only through the gifts from the holy one
Who charted the course and cemented the way
Through the life and death of the Son
That changes lives and makes them whole each passing day.

I have said these things to you, that in Me you may have peace. In the world you will have tribulation. But take heart; I have overcome the world.

—John 16:33

Faith Though Fear Remain

Lord, I am unsettled in this moment
Yet I delight simply to be in Your presence.
Not a word or request to utter
Just an acknowledgment that You are my cover

A shield to protect from the wind and rain
A hedge that blocks out the true effect of pain
My friend and confidant
Though I am not worthy of the love You grant.

Even in life's disappointments
You show up in ways to dispel and cast out the enemy's delusions
And in the mist of my dismay and discontent
The holy one never strays or wavers.
That is true commitment

To seek out my wondering soul
To save, keep, encourage, and hold
Close to the embers that will never cease
A burning seal to acknowledge the truth
And a destination that is resting in You.

Be strong and courageous. Do not fear or be in dread of them, for it is the LORD your God who goes with you. He will not leave you or forsake you.

—Deuteronomy 31:6

Forward with Boldness of Faith

Out of my fear movements are frozen
Even with the gentle nudging from heaven.
The reality is there is nothing to fear of loving;
It was showered upon His created and chosen.

Move me, oh Lord, beyond my hesitancy
Toward the direction that You have for me.
Shroud only in the light of Your mercy and grace
Then the fear and wavering move back behind me in its proper place.

Onward with boldness and vigilance
Upright with the wings of a true embrace
One that nothing and no one can erase
A life beyond the earthly existence
A choice made by some and avoided by many.

When your steps are guided by the holy one
Away with fears grip.
In boldness march forward and onward
And down comes the enemy's strongholds
Only faith in God will help carry the load.

And those who know Your name put their trust in You, for You, O LORD, have not forsaken those who seek You.

—Psalm 9:10

Walking Without Wavering

IT IS NOT in the law that comes love. It is the love proven in Jesus's walk and grace expressed in the interactions with others during the fulfillment of the law. How we treat one another is vital in relationships. Our actions should never focus solely on self or others' weaknesses or flaws. During my high school years, there were formal courses that all students had to pass to meet the minimum requirements for a high school diploma. The courses included attaining multiple credits in English, Math, Social Studies, History, and Government. The most pivotal lesson that has stuck with me from those classes occurred during my twelfth-grade US Government class.

In the class, we learned the branches of government and the responsibilities of each toward lawmaking. The teacher required everyone to stand up at the front of the classroom. We students were directed to stretch out our arms to create space between each other that was equivalent to an arm's length in distance from one another. The teacher instructed all of us to close our arms to the point that our fingers were almost touching our noses. As each student stood there, the teacher began to explain that there were limits to individual rights and actions. An individual's rights ended where another individual's rights began. You see, the arm's-length distance was the space between the students standing at the head of the class; however, when the hand of one student crossed the space and came strikingly close to the body of another student, that student's rights ended.

To respect the other person in a relationship, the parties in the relationship must acknowledge that there are rules of engagement that harness desires, will, and actions that must never overtake the other person. Because this action is so very distant from most human beings' ideology concerning life, it is difficult and sometimes draining to show this fundamental element of a healthy existence that places no harness on individual selflessness. We only have to view the content on all the media outlets to see how we take our words in the place of our hands to overtake others. Greater love has no one than this, that someone lay down his life for his friends (John 15:13). May the writings that follow encourage mindful reflection for a transition back to respect and the true value of a life.

Christ Will Sustain

A proclamation of sovereignty
A name given greater than ever will be
For a Savior nothing short of pure majesty
Beyond the imaginable for you and me.

Savior, Counselor, mighty Prince of Peace
Even more so for those that cannot see
A promise made so long ago
With an abundance of forgiveness, grace, and mercy.

To seek out and save even the one of those
Lost in a wilderness seeking their true home,
But what of the many in the search?
For they must forge on the path in the face of the thirst.

Even when the sky turns dark shades of gray
And it appears that the fear will overtake us each day,
Stay wrapped in the faith that the promise remains
And believe and trust that Christ will sustain.

Count it all joy, my brothers, when you meet trials of various kinds, for you know that the testing of your faith produces steadfastness. And let steadfastness have its full effect, that you may be perfect and complete, lacking in nothing.

—James 1:2–4

Looking Behind the Treasures

In the creation was the earth formed and shaped into being
Until the day of our ancestors' deceiving
A power far beyond that which our feeble hands can achieve
But only through the Master's speaking.

Where are your treasures?
In this life, laid up in houses and land
Or better yet, held tightly in your hands.
These are the treasures that will evaporate and fade away
Just as the earth is destined one day.

The impact of sin that rots to the core
Just as Abel's blood screamed as it permeated the soil,
An enemy so cunning and hard at work
Because in him no truth, humility, or concern, hiding in plain view.

Sin has as it was then and continues today
A destructive happening to earth and mankind
That we can overcome if we but pray.
And then in the horizon a new earth and heaven above
Will await those that through the wait have truly loved.

Blessed is the one who finds wisdom, and the one who gets understanding, for the gain from her is better than gain from silver and her profit better than gold. She is more precious than jewels, and nothing you desire can compare with her.

—Proverbs 3:13–15

Peace in the Season

For the Lord Himself imparts peace,
If we have peace
We have true relief
In this thing where time and space
Seek to alter, change, and erase

The very essence and meaning for Christ in this place.
No structure from the ten
But volumes of others to disguise
The enemy's divisive plans.

And where are they found,
Those to stand on higher ground?
Ah, in the fold of the popular vote
Forgetting the true value of each soul for the enemy's win.

Yet the promises are still rooted
For those who continue to stand
Upright and holding on
To the Master's hand.

No, in all these things we are more than conquerors through Him who loved us. For I am sure that neither death nor life, nor angels nor rulers, nor things present nor things to come, nor powers, nor height nor depth, nor anything else in all creation, will be able to separate us from the love of God in Christ Jesus our Lord.

—Romans 8:37–39

Ransom Paid

From the raw earth
A vessel created to carry a king
Shaped and formed
Free from all inequity
No movement or knowledge
Till the breath placed within,

For even at that time
The end of life's race.
Depicted and resolution to win
Man was given the opportunity

To hold fast to His Word.
Yet in the mist of decision
Picked up an imitating sword
Hiding the true wish to kill the love from the King.

Their hands marred with the rust from rotting metal
Visible for all to look upon in dismay
Looking into tomorrow steps in
The Master with patience, mercy, and grace.

Delivered the ultimate of sacrifice in correction
All to save man's biggest indiscretion
For the ancients and all would one day see
The fulfillment of destiny
Through the birth life and death of the Son of the King.

For I know that through your prayers and the help of the Spirit of Jesus Christ this will turn out for my deliverance.

—Philippians 1:19

Restoration Still Lives

God restores in so many ways
Over and over each day
From heartaches that were intended
To capture innocence and joy.

Through disillusion that praying brings no value anymore
As situations seemingly doomed without change
And life rolls on while the family unit
Becomes broken and continues to wain.

Outwardly good soldiers so many instances of death
Close friends and family members alike
Each one causing grief and some even strife
While these happenings though painful and disheartening at first sight
To find glory through the muddy water.

Seemingly brutal and strange
Is the greater of all falsities
Because God's love does not change
Some answers come swiftly with continuous praying tongues.

Others emerge, just not always what we would choose or want
Yet His love is never-ending and will cover the storms of life
Even when it seems that nothing
Will ever again be found right.

But they who wait for the LORD shall renew their strength; they shall mount up with wings like eagles; they shall run and not be weary; they shall walk and not faint.

—Isaiah 40:31

Sabbath Rest

His mercy and grace are not fleeting;
Our loss of trust in His presence is the reason
When life spins with difficulties
We find ourselves encouraged only by our worries and feelings.

Even though these times are not to be taken as a mystery
As they were spoken before.
Still, for many, overcoming is lost by the seeing
This place, if found there, has no permanency
Unless we choose to rest in that season.

His spoken word says six days of work at our being
And one special day to recharge and step away for healing,
A time to reclaim, recharge, and meditate
Reflect on His mercies and His grace
And the gifts granted to endure the journey and race.

One person esteems one day as better than another, while another esteems all days alike. Each one should be fully convinced in his own mind.

—Romans 14:5

The Breath Given

The breath You have given today
How will we react; will we obey?
With one step in front of the other
We have already been given
All that is needed for the perfect decision.

We reason and say, nothing is a given
But help us to not forget His precious birth, life, and death.
Nothing else is important
Only to walk in the victory won
Push past the dread of the season.

These words to some are cliche, redundant, and maybe even frivolous,
But to the one that has the Father, Son, and Spirit,
There is nothing more important and deliberate.
Take heed; watch, wait, and listen.

There will be a never-ending climax
That will move the unreachable into our vision.
Be intentional, humble, and faithful
And continue to walk with an understanding
That mercy, grace, and an agape love the I Am have given.

So now faith, hope, and love abide, these three; but the greatest of these is love.

—1 Corinthians 13:13

The Glory in the Veil

When the veil falls in this realm
Though brief it can sometimes be
Keeping the heart in tune perfects the vision to allow us to see
The stretch of His hand into the darkness.

Not pulling or tugging on thee
Just within our reach
Though cloudy the veil is purposeful to be
To blur the fingertips of His Majesty.

Still, He waits for us patiently
No forced confessions
Or guilted apologies
He only seeks that which was always His
Just an open-heart forgoing its will to lead.

Step by step, He will guide us through
But we can only see if a mustard seed measure of faith is true.
Time and time again the enemy attempts to assail
The glory in this, he also is constrained by the veil.

The race is not to the swift, nor the battle to the strong, nor bread to the wise, nor riches to the intelligent, nor favor to those with knowledge, but time and chance happen to them all.

—Ecclesiastes 9:11

The Morning Dew

The one, I Am, and Omega,
Father, Son, and Savior
It was that way before the earth was begun.
No sickness, pestilence, or death will change it.
These are only illusions to create mass confusion

Making our choices seemingly limited
When the Master has already won.
We have but to focus thoughts on the Son
Mimicking a life with no corruptions
A soul pre-ordained to meet all trials and tribulations.

For us, the life was given
The Word became flesh and proven
No longer a dream nor delusion
A message that your efforts though compelling for many no victory
We have but to believe and take care in our choosing.

Love one another as He loved us
Even when the same is not returned.
The way seems cloudy and out of view
For then the Lord steps in
As a light for our paths
And refreshes our hearts like the morning dew.

Commit your way to the LORD; trust in Him, and He will act. He will bring forth your righteousness as the light, and your justice as the noonday.

—Psalm 37:5–6

Value of My Portion

To each of us granted a part.
Do you value, cherish, and multiply its measure
Or does it sit in the jar on the shelf
As if fright to invest value and treasure?

Was it left to fend on its own
Without fertile soil to slowly wither and fade
As the locust conspicuously plucked and carried it away?

Is it growing beyond its shell and sphere
Flourishing and encouraging all that grow near
Toward an inner glow that draws
Even when the black hole descends?

Does it show the Father's investment
A value beyond any to receive
Was accepted and produced fruits
Worthy to that of the sons and daughters of the true King?

Looking to Jesus, the founder and perfecter of our faith, who for the joy that was set before Him endured the cross, despising the shame, and is seated at the right hand of the throne of God.

—Hebrews 12:2

When Faith Is Lost

Where God's grace abounds
And He is omnipotent and benevolent
With a genuine love for us
That has no bounds

Shares of His love so equally placed
As He showers us daily with new mercies
Beyond the tragedy of this world's embrace
More than we can ever begin to imagine.

No chatter from the stones can erase
All but to lavish in His very presence
For the latter victory of walking
And talking with the Father, Son, and Spirit
A chance to see the Master's face.

So why leave so much to chance
When the race has already been foretold?
It is not one answer but many
Because the enemy is relentless in building strongholds

Just as the mighty King clipped the wings of the serpent
So shall the end come to all that have tried to usurp Him.
To not be numbered among the tragic is my goal.
Ask yourselves a question, my dear friend:
Is any of this truly worth losing your soul?

God gave us a spirit not of fear but of power and love and self-control.

—2 Timothy 1:7

Faith Undivided

The measure of one's faith cannot be taught;
Yes, the price was paid, and debt bought.
All that is left is to trust and obey
For the victory is not just for the former but today.

Live life in the newness of discovery
That through the Savior's death is our recovery.
All that was lost in a garden far away
Not a sigh, frown, or inkling of dismay.

To think, do, and say are all that is needed
To display a faith that is not mired
By the stains that were intended
When the sins of the enemy descended.

Yet so many fall prey with unbridled senses
To a world that has no use for sons and daughters of glory.
Yet these are they that when ignited
Exemplify in action and deed a faith that is undivided.

So, faith comes from hearing, and hearing through the Word of Christ.
—Romans 10:17

Choices

The choices we make are important;
They frame the outline of our story.
From the beginning the pages were filled with losses and wins,
And it will continue until the very ending.

The focus for us is not to attain riches untold
But to live a life that follows the respective path to save the soul.
His primary mission
To bridge the partition

That separated us from the Master.
Through the skeleton and flesh
Misery and anguish tarnished away,
Never to appear again after the day
But wait; that is the latter.

For right now is the present;
Wait, watch, pray, and pay close attention.
We are all part of the glorious mission
Strive for existence full of joy and laughter.

For if not, we sink into mind-accepted disaster;
To avoid this fate
Requires our mental presence
To truly see in God's eye what really matters.

And whatever you ask in prayer, you will receive, if you have faith.

—Matthew 21:22

Christ's Life Is the Way

Love is not easy when you must think about it:
Thoughts make you focus on the unimportant things
The he-said-she-said mutterings
You know; the words, acts, and deeds born from frustration.

To think too long, hard, or much
May pass the opportunity for the Master's touch,
For He is all the love we need
To cure the wretchedness of the hatred disease.

March as you do, sing as you can, shout loud enough
Yet no true change in the inner man.
How can this be, together we move to try and pave the way
For things to be better than yesterday.

It is not the who, what, or when;
No earthly thing has the fortitude to change the sky from gray
That is only found in the trueness
And power in knowing
Christ is the Life that paved the way.

For we are his workmanship, created in Christ Jesus for good works, which God prepared beforehand, that we should walk in them.

—Ephesians 2:10

A Forever Kind of Love

Give thanks with a purposeful mind
Stayed on the Master in all seasons each one in kind.
Where the treasure laid up lies,
Will thy true faith reveal in time?

When facing the day-to-day
Our purpose is clear
Actions toward others be justly
Only notes of loving kindness without fear.

In the most challenging times
And yes, they will appear,
Especially with those bent on distress
And seedlings of angry tears.

Humbly walk in the presence
Of His Holy Spirit to intentional reliance
That releases the armor
Of comfort, grace, mercy, and good cheer.

Many are the plans in the mind of a man, but it is the purpose of the LORD that will stand.

—Proverbs 19:21

To Be Righteous

If I were righteous,
It would not matter what you think of me
'Cause your thoughts are surface-level.
I would know they are only what the eyes perceive to be.

If I were righteous,
It would not matter the lot assigned to me
'Cause any lot that comes from the Lord
Is nothing short of a masterpiece.

If I were righteous,
It would only matter what you felt from me,
For in His presence a tiny vessel
Shining His marvelous light is what I would be.

I want to be righteous
'Cause that is what Gods seeks from me,
The power He granted through the Son on Calvary
Oh, to be His righteous is what I strive to be.

Enter by the narrow gate. For the gate is wide and the way is easy that leads to destruction, and those who enter by it are many. For the gate is narrow and the way is hard that leads to life, and those who find it are few.

—Matthew 7:13–14

We Are Not Our Own

In frivolity we place our strength
In the heart's cares and mental contents
While yet uniquely we are in this existence
Some with greater lots and positions.

In reality, the heart is the same
Unless a force seeks to change
Far beyond the treks to outer space
And the ingenuity that we may embrace.

The lifeless glitter and glamour of it all
Gains in wealth and prosperity
Never again to control the trajectory
None of it will be taken at the last call.

Yet when the clock tolls not one of them gone
Could tell the remaining what to make of it all
A constant turn of life's spinning wheel
Even in calamity the enemy's forces seek to conceal.

Yet the Father has a master plan
That is available to every man
If only the faith were strong enough to lay claim
Instead of seeking the vapor found in the enemy's reign.

Jesus said to them, I am the bread of life; whoever comes to Me shall not hunger, and whoever believes in Me shall never thirst.

—John 6:35

When Darkness Presses Down

Although each day is a struggle,
Some are so much more difficult than others.
Faith if greater than a sandy grain
Is all that is needed to carry us through.

Even when darkness is pressing down
And all the host of them hanging around,
There is always a path to calm the noise
That the enemy purposes to bring to me and you:

A noise so deafening at times
With purpose to try to take sight
With subtle suggestions for us to give up
And give in to his way of life.

That is not the ending for those intentional
While in those moments seek His Word and face.
Take counsel in that which is from the Master;
Be intentional in purpose to feed the mind and wait and watch
As the Lord navigates us above and through and out.

Trust in the LORD with all your heart, and do not lean on your own understanding.

—Proverbs 3:5

We Can Command

Everyone has a journey to take,
And as the breath of life remain decisions to make.
They come in many shapes and forms;
Some are strictly earthly-based.

For those take due caution
To not worry and become all-consumed
As they are distractions with not one added day
Only pathways to destruction and gloom,

Grab hold to the Master's hand
For guidance and protection of the inner man
With purposeful intentions forward and upward
Toward heavenly dimensions.

When placing such high priority,
There is the strength to withstand
Anything the enemy devises and not in God's plans.
It is the part of the journey that seems to cause time to stand still.

While we deal with the chaos
That appears to happen at will
Not our job to understand the what, why, or when
Through the Father, Son, and Spirit,
Even these times we can command.

May the God of hope fill you with all joy and peace in believing, so that by the power of the Holy Spirit you may abound in hope.

—Romans 15:13

The Breath of Life

Live each day with new breath
For tomorrow is not promised
And might not present opportunities as today
Though come as it may.

We have but one certainty
And that is the moment we are in
And do visibly see
That what the Lord gives is far bigger than anything from you and me.

So, for some knowing all of this is true
Why do we seemingly stick like glue
To the earthly things that will in the day
Become combustible and waste away?

Our love and trust misplaced
In the things that are to be erased
No grounding and rooting for His powerful love
Or fear of missing the blessing of His mercy and grace
Better yet, seeing the I Am face to face.

Now faith is the assurance of things hoped for, the conviction of things not seen. For by it the people of old received their commendation.

—Hebrews 11:1–2

PART III:
Journey Through the Unknown

FOR MANY, FINDING one's purpose is overshadowed by everyday life occurrences. The grooming that occurs from child to adulthood leaves little opportunity for spiritual mindedness. The focus is placed on achievement either physically, mentally, socially, or financially. From the time a child is introduced to the concept that there are other entities on this earth besides him or herself, the competition begins. After the cradle, there is competition for the parents' attention. Introduction to systemic learning inspires competition among friends. At the work site, competing for financial superiority takes shape. In our homes, when the competition years should wain, there is keeping up with the Joneses next door. In these are the examples of deviations from true purpose. We only have to look to the Lord to see the importance of living out true purpose without deviation. Jesus, as the very essence of God, never counted Himself equal to God simply because of who He was as described in Philippians 2:3. He emptied himself and became a devoted servant to God to learn how to serve and live out God's purpose for us through His life. With passion and fervor, Jesus journeyed with conviction for His purpose.

We see the imagery of the one monumental act; however, our God is intricately complex, and yet, the woven fabric of Jesus's life exemplifies truly abiding in and living out God's spoken and written law so very simple and plain. This fabric becomes the blueprint for how we can follow in the footsteps of Jesus. Galatians 5:22–23 summarizes the confirmation that will be shown in our lives of a house built on a solid foundation. The author presents contextual aspects of a house that is not manufactured by earthly means but guided by heavenly principles that will be unshakeable, unmovable, and that includes individuals who sojourn through life with intentional choices to accept the will of God and receive these attributes (love, joy, peace, forbearance, kindness, goodness, faithfulness, gentleness, and self-control). The frequency of occurrence in the Scriptures might suggest a hierarchy of importance among these attributes, as love is referenced more often than any other.

Conviction to Love

CONVICTION IS DEFINED as the process of a person being convinced of an error or an oversight (Merriam-Webster, 2022). Imagine the power of change that might result if all people were convicted of their errors when it comes to expressions of love. I think back to my early years in my career when a manager had the opportunity to pour expressions of positivity and love in my life. It was during the annual performance evaluation, when I was told that I was no more than a worker, not of management material or promotable, just a good worker. This person had no idea what those comments fueled in my life. In response to the lack of positive expression, I purposed to prove the statements were false and went on to show excellence in management and leadership while pursuing my own personal growth opportunities. *Moving forward* are two words that are a call to action that sometimes seem insurmountable. Defeated minds give hold to the negativity in the mountain. It is at those times that the believer must center the mind and get to a place where the insurmountable becomes the unseen.

To focus time and effort on what appears so highly likely gives power to being defeated. I always thought at some time in the future, if ever I had the opportunity, I would boldly confront the individual of the error in that person's connection point in my life. However, when the opportunity presented itself, I saw the frailty of the stature of the individual and merely focused on pouring love into that person's situation. The word *conviction* is pregnant with meaning. Yet, in our choices, our actions demonstrate our abilities to move forward despite what may be designed to derail us in this space. We are in an age in which it has become the norm for all people to speak *their truths*. The problem with this new norm is *your truth* is not always *the truth*. Your truth is influenced by your worldview. Your worldview will affect how the challenge comes alive for you and your response to the challenge. This next series of writings are to encourage reflection of your conviction and where your passion truly lies in this life.

Coming into View

He said it with conviction
One day no more to carry
As His purpose was fulfilled
We who were left to tarry.

The truth is not hidden from us
The veil may obscure the view
Just as mountains rise high in the distance
The peaks will eventually perforate through.

The valley may appear endless
Many a change in season with no advance,
Beloved, rest and be assured
The walk is not in a single stance.

The steps are ordered, and advancement is sure
As day after day moving one in front of the other
Giving uncertainty no power
A clearing from the perfect will emerges into our view.

Do not be conformed to this world, but be transformed by the renewal of your mind, that by testing you may discern what is the will of God, what is good and acceptable and perfect.

—Romans 12:2

Deliverance

My deliverance is not for everyone
That journey is specifically for me
No matter the difference in roads traveled
The Savior will find and lead thee.

Through the storm
No matter the severity
His serving spirit awaits the decision
To follow all the way toward peace.

Though the view is sometimes skewed
The form and shape beyond the visible
I know He is there for me
And nothing from the journey is foreign to thee.

My choice, my life all the way
My decision and my view
Are beyond what you think and perceive for me;
They are reaching out for the love of the Father
That is available for all to receive.

Even though I walk through the valley of the shadow of death, I will fear no evil, for You are with me; Your rod and Your staff, they comfort me. You prepare a table before me in the presence of my enemies; You anoint my head with oil; my cup overflows. Surely goodness and mercy shall follow me all the days of my life, and I shall dwell in the house of the LORD forever.

—Psalm 23:4–6

In the Promises

The Lord is still my covering,
Though sometimes the day becomes night
And it seems to drown out His calling,
And sometimes yields clouds and rain.

The eve smothered in heartache and pain,
He will never leave or cease to be the Comforter,
Although we often walk from under His protective covering,
We have only to call upon His holy name.

The only one who genuinely cares,
He has promised,
And the ancients foretold,
How He purposed to seek out the lost

And save the worst of us wondering souls.
So, why so distressed with the level of chaos and earthly duress
When the Master has proven Himself to be the same
Yesterday, today, and will be even through the next storm and rain?

But God shows His love for us in that while we were still sinners, Christ died for us.

—Romans 5:8

Live Like Only Today

The treasure for obedience
Does not rest in the visible.
We can only imagine what awaits
The heart that is pure.
A mind filled with focus

And trust in the one:
A Creator, a Son, and the Holy Spirit.
The Word from spoken, written to live
How do we respond?
Will our hearts be fulfilled?

A journey that tests
Our very essence and will,
Though wide and rugged
Sometimes is the terrain,
Narrow the path we must navigate.

Let go of ours
And seek His will to sustain.
What awaits each passing day
Cannot be decided,

Only the choices and responses,
The many successes and failures,
All gifts along the way.
Tomorrow was never promised.
Live and love like we have only today.

Whatever you do, work heartily, as for the Lord and not for men, knowing that from the Lord you will receive the inheritance as your reward.

—Colossians 3:23–24

Overflow Through the Struggle

The power does not come from the done
Yet the struggle continues beyond.
Knowing the true meaning
The measure of truth and life within
Is the source that many have yet to receive it.

Though this be the case
And confusion cloud the view
More and more each day
There is still an appointed time and place
To complete what was once begun.

In unison, the *we* created all
With a single purpose
A fellowship, kinship, and family
Not to be confused by false deities.

Even so came the event to try to shatter it all;
No grief for the broken pieces
From whatever the reason
With the living water.

The hardened clay
If accepted on the appointed day
Will be molded once again
As if no effect from the fall.

Therefore, if anyone is in Christ, he is a new creation. The old has passed away; behold, the new has come. All this is from God, who through Christ reconciled us to Himself and gave us the ministry of reconciliation; that is, in Christ, God was reconciling the world to Himself, not counting their trespasses against them, and entrusting to us the message of reconciliation.

—2 Corinthians 5:17–19

The Samaritan's Example

The knocks and bruises of this life
Are constantly rearing their ugly heads,
Like the man robbed beaten and left for dead.
What did the legals perceive to be best?

Those that could help did not
And marched away with weighted chest.
Along comes the Samaritan
To pick up the broken

Piece after piece along the way
Inserted his bones for the tokens
A ransom that only a true king could pay
When all others simply moved and ran away.

With no remorse or care, thank Christ for His grace
And the mercy He shared to a dying world.
He is the example to follow
To avoid being caught up in the enemy's snare.

For this is the will of my Father, that everyone who looks on the Son and believes in Him should have eternal life, and I will raise him up on the last day.

—John 6:40

The Ten

In this dimension, none before Thee
No life, thing, place, or liberty
No imagery of the Creator and powers that be
From the eye here these shall not us see.
A precious name take not in vain
For this a true sin to thee.
A day set to remember the time spent just for you and me
Reflecting upon His love, grace, and mercy
To honor the two above all, extends beyond what we can hope to see.
No death in word or deed must a focus be
End thoughts of idolatry
Included in these is the purposeful intent.
Not to take, steal away, or break
The spirit that exists from any of them.

For the wages of sin is death, but the free gift of God is eternal life in Christ Jesus our Lord.

—Romans 6:23

Walking in Rain

The toll of sin was so great
No earthly sacrifice or work could erase
A stain that required the ultimate cleanse
A life lived, sacrifice and death
Not of the soul but the iniquities of the flesh.

A piercing of the side and release of pure blood
That covered a multitude of evil and bad with ultimate good.
Now we that walk are held by grace and mercy
Yet many do not understand that even to this will come an end.

For what is left for one to contemplate life for now only
Pursuit of riches and fame
Living life with unforgiveness and pain
Or seek to discover the endless bounty that awaits.

The one who strives to walk the narrow path to one day see His face
When we strive for the latter
Surely, we understand that this road will not be easy
There will be continual struggles and stress.

Only through the Master's great plan
Will we be able to stand and know
How to weather each storm
To pass the next test.

If you abide in Me, and My words abide in you, ask whatever you wish, and it will be done for you.

—John 15:7

Victory Is Ours

We struggle for many reasons,
Some because we want more than we have in the season,
Others because we have far more than we can handle,
Not enough, too little, yet we think these are valid reasons.

Still there is another group of us who are yet in neither category.
Who accept the station we are in
Giving bountiful thanks to the Lord above
For He knows what is best for our being.

Examine yourself this very day
Be on guard for the attack and assail
Live life with a heart in the right place
Turn away from the pressure to give in
For this life is not a sprint or quick race.

During the struggle for true strength
There is only one origin:
Reach out for the One who has already won
There you will find your victory in His win.

They are to do good, to be rich in good works, to be generous and ready to share, thus storing up treasure for themselves as a good foundation for the future, so that they may take hold of that which is truly life.

—1 Timothy 6:18–19

The Unending Reign

While yet the locusts eat away
God's love is eternal and here to stay.
We only must wait, watch, and pray
Spending holy time in His Word each day.

Those are the embers to stoke the fire
That calm creeping deathly desires
Shroud in stress worry and carelessness
Of people places and things that increasingly mean less and less.

Even when they surround us day in and out
Smothering and suffocating the mind's true might
To identify and see the gifts planted within
To be used to turn just one from sin.

That are disguised by the working of the enemy
In the pleasure of all things that will come to an ending
No notoriety will defame, nor money can refrain,
The second coming of the one true King and His unending reign.

And without faith it is impossible to please Him, for whoever would draw near to God must believe that He exists and that He rewards those who seek Him.

—Hebrews 11:6

Way of Escape

THE HOLY SCRIPTURES describe one miracle performed by the Master as the surgical repair of Malchus's ear (Matt. 26:51; Mark 14:47; Luke 22:50–51; John 18:10–11). From certain vantage points of these verses, one might posit that this action was the preservation of Peter's innocence from a deed that was surely to result in his execution alongside Jesus or sometime thereafter. For a moment, I challenge us to also consider that of all of the latter miracle deeds and actions taken upon the precipice of knowing that His life would surely be coming to its full purpose, there was not an act to forcibly remove the scales from His antagonists' eyes toward His favor, but an act of love and preservation for the ages to come. From this humble servant's worldview, Christ, after foretelling Peter of his actions, saved him. Even when Jesus knew Peter would deny Him, His action was full acceptance of Peter as one of His own to be kept and saved. At that point in time, Jesus could have pleaded with the Father to make time stand still, obliterate every breath around Him, and ask for a new plan for Himself, but no, His conviction was sealed in providing the way of escape, that is still ours to walk in today. There is something to be said about being in the right place at the right time. Malchus, too, received a blessing, simply because Jesus was nearby.

Often today, we celebrate the headlines of perceived heroic deeds and actions that pale in comparison to the sacrifice that is exemplified in the life, death, and resurrection of Christ. We assign immense value to individuals that speak their minds, amass great financial wealth, and collectors of worldly knowledge as deserving great praise and accolades. And yet, not one of them has the power to grant us everlasting life. As I look back on the journey of my life, I see all the roadblocks I caused, yet the Father still covered and preserved me. In the writings that follow, I pray we will be encouraged to seek out the one who loves unconditionally with the fiercest of convictions for those that are His.

Along the Journey

Sometimes the journey seems so very smooth;
There are no mountain peaks to climb
Or winding roads to deeper valleys below.
It is during these times we feel the greatest sense of being in tune
With our Lord and Savior.

How do we balance around the bend when Everest begins to descend?
Does the view of the road fade or disappear,
Or did we become too relaxed and consumed,
Let our guard down, thinking nothing contrary would once again come our way?

Where is the balance when we lose altitude?
The drop seems to take our very breath away
But for us, my friend is the I Am who is always here,
A treasure not hidden in the mountain peak or valley low.
He is the heart's keeper, guide, and friend.

To not wallow, tarry, or sink
Into the hillside is the goal.
Though the soil attempts to hold,
Plant your feet upon the smoothness in the memory
Of higher ground and smoother roads.

Behold, I stand at the door and knock. If anyone hears My voice and opens the door, I will come in to him and eat with him, and he with Me.

—Revelation 3:20

Carrying the Torch

It is no secret that when we look at others,
An extension of one's view of self invades.
For some, the physical attributes
Either magnify negative feelings

For our own internal perceptions
Or provide avenues for affirmation
Of perceived superior reflections
For whatever your imagery commands.

Never lose sight that our reaction
Though internally driven
Potentially places others
And their responses tied to our hands.

Responses that have lifelong implications
And soul trajectory navigations
That can quickly erase
The success of staying on plan.

Be ever vigilant, humble, and intentional
In your daily interactions,
For many near and far are watching to see
How a life succeeds in the journey
That is meant to carry the torch within.

So that Christ may dwell in your hearts through faith, that you, being rooted and grounded in love, may have strength to comprehend with all the saints what is the breadth and length and height and depth, and to know the love of Christ that surpasses knowledge, that you may be filled with all the fullness of God.

—Ephesians 3:17–19

Hold On to the Gift

Be careful, my friend,
That the choices we make
Will support the mission to win.
It will be a dreadful mistake

To lose the race
Simply because of giving in.
We are not alone in the struggle
Because God in His infinite wisdom

Paved a pathway upon the stones
That leads to His kingdom.
If we choose to not give in
Through this road to recovery

Includes the wonderous walk for us
With a guiding light of true discovery
For the abundant gifts He has placed
To let us know we are not alone.

Though try as the enemy may
To wreak havoc and spoils for each day,
Christ's win through the span of His life
Assured for us a fixed fight
That will not be undone.

Be careful, my friend,
Be present in each day
Minds clearly focused on the mission
Claiming the victory
For the race already won.

Father, I desire that they also, whom You have given Me, may be with Me where I am, to see My glory that You have given Me because You loved Me before the foundation of the world.

—John 17:24

Kept in Christ

What I have to offer
Is not what You request of me
Only that in my being I seek to be
In alignment with Your perfect will
For that is where my gifts I truly see.

To be of service along the journey
And be found within the seam of the fold
Where life begins and death has no hold
Dear Lord, open my mind that I may yearn to be
Exactly what You would have of me.

Though right now the pathway seems unclear
I thank you, Lord, for always being here.
Your loving Spirit to direct my steps
My comforter, friend, and Savior in You my soul is kept.

Away in the realms where vision cannot travel
Through the thickness of the veil that cannot be simply unraveled
A deep intentional connection with the Master,
I know, is the only prescription for the appearance of earthly born disaster.

I have been crucified with Christ. It is no longer I who live, but Christ who lives in me. And the life I now live in the flesh I live by faith in the Son of God, who loved me and gave Himself for me. I do not nullify the grace of God, for if righteousness were through the law, then Christ died for no purpose.

—Galatians 2:20–21

Matchless Love

I pray these words are not a thorn
Or become misunderstood.
Even the best athletes must work hard at their crafts
To run the risk of not being great but just ordinarily good.

The seasons we have are by no means guaranteed
For many the best times of life are spent on bended knees
In fellowship with the true director of their journeys
In heartfelt submission to the perfecting teachings of what will give life eternal.

A hard message for some wrapped in the day-to-day
Consumed by things and all that people say
To exist beyond all that we see
Is a remarkable feat for you and me.

This too takes a focused goal
To accept the peace of life
As the guardian of your soul
And relinquish the familiar or what seems reality.

For in this action there are requirements to be kept
To live and love all His children
Beyond our faults and shortcomings
Just as His matchless love was expressed in the beginning.

Always carrying in the body, the death of Jesus, so that the life of Jesus may also be manifested in our bodies.

—2 Corinthians 4:10

Moving through This Season

Yesterday is a memory;
Tomorrow is not promised.
Right now is your time
Seek your peace and joy
This is your season.

Purpose your steps
To abide in His mercy and grace.
Rely on the Holy Spirit to guide you through this space.
Right now is your time
Seek your peace and joy.
This is your season.

Rest in His victory
Live in the newness of knowing His love endures all.
His mercy and grace are sufficient to carry us through this time and place.
Right now is your time.
Seek your peace and joy
This is your season.

Give thanks and rejoice
For through it all was revealed a battle already won
A victory you can claim
If only a heart that is pure
And rests within His strength to endure.
Right now is your time.
Seek your peace and joy
This is your season.

But you are a chosen race, a royal priesthood, a holy nation, a people for His own possession, that you may proclaim the excellencies of Him who called you out of darkness into His marvelous light.

—1 Peter 2:9

Nothing of This Earth Saves

For some, the crushing comes tenfold
They cannot seem to understand
They have become jaded
Because of too many things at hand.

Still the lighter does not one make innocent
For in their condition
To advance to another station
Reach they for artificial soul senses and stimulations.

Others simply check out
As if no care or concerns
Mind's eye very consumed
With many addictions
Shroud in the enemy's afflictions.

They drown in the *whys* and what else is left to do?
Eyes off the Master
In either be us found
Focusing solely on self and others
Is a plan meant for disaster
And to nowhere be bound.

Be of good cheer whatever station in life
Be thankful if less headache and strife
Work as if the greatest has been granted
And never lose true sight.

On a camel or donkey, make sure your election is true;
There is but one Master
Nothing of this earth
Neither land nor riches will do.

For we are His workmanship, created in Christ Jesus for good works, which God prepared beforehand, that we should walk in them.

—Ephesians 2:10

Provision of Grace

For in this realm
We find ourselves physically bound
Until the Master returns
Or our journey comes to its conclusion.

At this turn, what words to utter
A life exemplified of happiness, peace, joy, and love,
Or the latter of sadness, worry, stress,
and separation from above.

So many things are uncertain
With every new day granted
We must take heed and be guarded in decisions.
For to squander away

That which was granted
By mercy and grace
Cannot be reclaimed
At the end of the season.

For everything there is a season, and a time for every matter under heaven: a time to be born, and a time to die; a time to plant, and a time to pluck up what is planted; a time to kill, and a time to heal; a time to break down, and a time to build up; a time to weep, and a time to laugh; a time to mourn, and a time to dance; a time to cast away stones, and a time to gather stones together; a time to embrace, and a time to refrain from embracing; a time to seek, and a time to lose; a time to keep, and a time to cast away; a time to tear, and a time to sew; a time to keep silence, and a time to speak; a time to love, and a time to hate; a time for war, and a time for peace.

—Ecclesiastes 2:25–3:8

Simply Walk Away

Life brings so many positive and negative things;
To each there is a response.
Do our first actions embody
That of being a child of the King,

Foregoing boastings and frivolous words
In favor of the stillness that being humble brings?
Though sometimes the challenges become so great,
It is far better to turn and walk away

Than to stay and fight with no ammunition
Because Jesus requires thoughtful and guided intention.
Pain blurs the subject matter,
Frustration veils the true enemy,

Confusion shrouds the solution
To make us lose poise and position,
Moving away from the safety of heavenly resolutions,
That are required for everything.

A heart carved from the clay
Focused and determined to see souls saved
To stand upright to a world that so desperately needs to see
The Jesus in you and me.

The Lord is not slow to fulfill His promise as some count slowness, but is patient toward you, not wishing that any should perish, but that all should reach repentance.

—2 Peter 3:9

Speckled, Spotted, and Striped

Speckled, spotted, and striped
Each day many of us walk through this life.
Imperfection and human frailties
None too much for the Lord's might.

Should our condition never change and take flight,
The Lord will continue to guide us
Even in the darkest hour of night.
For whatsoever our lot,

We can rest assured
The battle is already won.
For this earthly fight
Our part it is still true.

To experience the workings of God
Is a part of the journey too,
Not for the sake of punishment or dowry
But our crosses visible to all that He carries.

On our own we are sure to falter
Merely from the weight of the load.
Seek joy over happiness,
One is yesterday, today, or never,
The other abides in the soul.

The LORD is my Light and my salvation; whom shall I fear? The LORD is the stronghold of my life; of whom shall I be afraid?

—Psalm 27:1

Under Heavenly Wings

Invest in a heavenly mindset
For there is everlasting joy and peace.
Focus each thought for the day
Using a strategic focus that turns the mind's eye
From disappointment and dismay.

Be of good cheer
Despite the spoils that each day may bring.
The question becomes
How do we continue to thrive
When others try to negatively impact our lives?

The clarity we need
Can only be found in one thing:
A walk with the heavenly Father
Along this journey to a better life,
Even with the negativity and strife.

We were destined to be one with the Master
Despite the first taste of disaster.
There is victory yet for you and for me
All but to claim it with a life
And choices that frame it.

This is my true lot
Not the superficial that earthly eyes can see
But an invisible invincible walk with the true King.
And when the turmoil abounds
For there is where I will strive to be found
Under the cover of heavenly wings.

Count it all joy, my brothers, when you meet trials of various kinds, for you know that the testing of your faith produces steadfastness.

—James 1:2–3

Time Is Not Lost

We are all in our respective places
On a journey that includes myriads of faces,
Yet although we are intertwined
Some are more tightly bound.

And to those we place grand expectations
Once they let us down
No more joy and peace are found
How quickly a loving heart the mind erases.

It was not the first plan
For the love and care to end,
Nor the existence of these frustrations
It was not meant to be at all this way.

Yet we find ourselves in a world
That is full of so much confusion
In this time and in so many places.
Is it all simply a grand illusion,
Or have we reached the pinnacle
Of something that has no positive conclusion?

No, my friend, that's the enemy's plan,
A calculated way to have us live,
As though each day is rainy
When God already reclaimed our ending.

For I consider that the sufferings of this present time are not worth comparing with the glory that is to be revealed to us.

—Romans 8:18

Thorny Blessings

If my thorns were removed and I freely navigate,
I dare say I would more likely lose sight of His face,
Not because He moves and repositions
Due to my own lawless compromises and daily omissions.

Each day would bring freedoms that abound
No conflicts, restrictions, or boundaries to remind me He is ever around.
No chance for His will and my works to conjoin
A life without the Master heading for final disaster

Because without His presence is the end of my very essence.
Paul knew it best though he pleaded for redress
To remove his thorn at first request.
After some conversation, it became evident
Though unknown, the thorn was a blessing.

A response so profound and intentional
To show the value in allowing the enemy's interventions
To allow me to see the bigger picture
That my salvation though freely given
Requires self-annihilation not in the physical but the temporal.

Every athlete exercises self-control in all things. They do it to receive a perishable wreath, but we an imperishable.

—1 Corinthians 9:25

Reflections

It is my prayer that the writings in this book move you toward mindful spiritualness in a way that elevates your consciousness from the temporary struggles of this world toward a conviction for the destination in Christ. As distractions abound for us each day beginning the moment we awaken, there are endless thoughts. This is so much so, that one day, I endeavored to paint an entire house because it was less of a struggle to see the paint brush go up and down and the color change on the walls than to sit down for a second of mental idleness. This we will unpack in another space and time, should it be the Lord's will and plan for my life.

About the Author

THE AUTHOR IS a humble servant of God that is seeking to lift up the Lord in this space, encourage anyone to increase the measure of faith given, and seek out and hold on to the Master's loving hand.

CPSIA information can be obtained
at www.ICGtesting.com
Printed in the USA
BVHW080049031222
653304BV00009B/902

9 781662 862977